The Secret Lives of Plants

Jill McDougall

The Secret Lives of Plants

Text: Jill McDougall
Publishers: Tania Mazzeo and Eliza Webb
Series consultant: Amanda Sutera
  Hands on Heads Consulting
Editor: Laken Ballinger
Project editor: Annabel Smith
Designer: Leigh Ashforth
Project designer: Danielle Maccarone
Illustrations: Claire McElfatrick
Permissions researcher: Helen Mammides
Production controller: Renee Tome

Acknowledgements
We would like to thank the following for permission to reproduce
copyright material:

Front cover: iStock.com/Rawpixel; pp. 1, 8: Shutterstock.com/Bess Hamitii;
p. 4: Getty Images/David Kirkland/Design Pics; p. 5 (top):
Shutterstock.com/Aoshi VN, (bottom): Shutterstock.com/LHBLLC; p. 7
(top): Shutterstock.com/Wolfen, (bottom): iStock.com/southtownboy; p. 9
(top): Shutterstock.com/Ruth Swan, (bottom): iStock.com/GuruJosh; p. 10
(top): Alamy Stock Photo/Reinhard Dirscherl, (bottom): Adobe Stock/
Paitoon; p. 11 (bottom): Alamy Stock Photo/Design Pics Inc; p. 12:
Shutterstock.com/Banonili; p. 14 (top): iStock.com/helivideo, (middle):
Shutterstock.com/Kuttelvaserova Stuchelova, (bottom): Shutterstock.com/
Maslov Dmitry; p. 15: Alamy Stock Photo/Gillian Pullinger; p. 16: Alamy
Stock Photo/Gretchen's Gallery; pp. 17 (top), 24: Shutterstock.com/
alohaisland, (bottom): Shutterstock.com/vilax; p. 19 (top right): Alamy
Stock Photo/Robert Wyatt; p. 20: Shutterstock.com/Lisa A. Ernst; p. 21
(top): iStock.com/PaulMaguire, (bottom): Shutterstock.com/picton; p. 22:
iStock.com/FatCamera; p. 23 (top): iStock.com/24K-Production, (bottom):
Alamy Stock Photo/Hero Images Inc; back cover (top): Shutterstock.com/
Protasov AN, (bottom): Shutterstock.com/Dewin ID.

Every effort has been made to trace and acknowledge copyright.
However, if any infringement has occurred, the publishers tender their
apologies and invite the copyright holders to contact them.

Novastar

Cengage Learning Australia
Level 5, 80 Dorcas Street
Southbank VIC 3006 Australia
Phone: 1300 790 853
Email: aust.nelsonprimary@cengage.com

For learning solutions, visit cengage.com.au

Printed in China by 1010 Printing International Ltd
1 2 3 4 5 6 7 28 27 26 25 24

*Nelson acknowledges the Traditional Owners and Custodians
of the lands of all First Nations Peoples. We pay respect
to Elders past and present, and extend that respect to
all First Nations Peoples today.*

Contents

Sneaky Plants

Plants – it's easy to think that they live boring lives. After all, plants don't seem to do much. They just stay in one place and grow slowly, right? Ha! Plants may look harmless, but don't be fooled. They will do whatever it takes to stay alive and **reproduce**.

You might be surprised by the secret lives of plants!

The rafflesia is the world's largest flower, and it smells horrible!

A lot of the food we eat comes from plants.

Plants like cacti can live in the driest places in the world.

Flower Power

Why do plants grow colourful flowers? Is it just so that we can admire them? Not at all! Flowers have an important job. They make seeds so that the plants can reproduce.

To make seeds, flowers need **pollen** from other plants. But if plants can't move from place to place, how do flowers get pollen?

Many flowers make **nectar** that **attracts** creatures like bees. When a bee lands on a flower, pollen sticks to its body. Then, when it visits the next flower, some pollen from the first flower falls off.

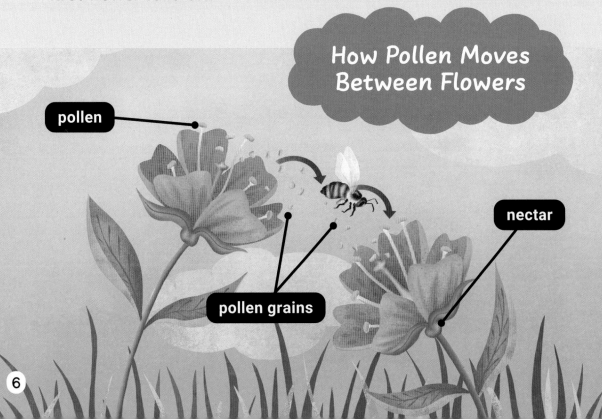

How Pollen Moves Between Flowers

pollen

pollen grains

nectar

Pollen sticks to bees as they drink from different flowers.

In this way, plants achieve **pollination**. Once flowers are pollinated, they can grow seeds, and that means lots of new plants!

New plants and flowers can grow when there are lots of creatures to pollinate them!

Seeds on the Move

Look around and you'll see that plants are everywhere. They can climb walls, grow in desert sand and even float about in the ocean. But how do plants get to so many different places?

Well, plants have some amazing ways of sending their seeds into the world. For example, each seed from a dandelion plant flies on fluffy threads shaped like a tiny parachute.

Seeds that Float Far

Dandelion seeds can float as far as 100 kilometres away from their plant.

Dandelion seeds float away from the flower when the wind blows.

And if you think a parachute is a clever idea, how about a helicopter? The seeds from a sycamore tree can spin in the air because they have wings that act like helicopter blades.

Sycamore seeds have two wings so they can spin through the air.

Sycamore trees grow lots of seeds that can grow new trees.

Some seeds are too heavy
to fly through the air, but they
can still find ways to move
around the world.

Coconuts are seeds from
a coconut palm tree.
When a coconut falls onto
a beach, it can be carried to
far-off places by the ocean.

Coconuts float in the ocean
to reach new places to grow.

Coconut palm trees grow coconuts,
which are seeds.

How a Coconut Floats

Air is trapped here.

Coconuts have air trapped inside, which allows them to float on the water.

When a coconut arrives on another shore, it can grow into a new coconut palm tree and make more coconuts.

This coconut is already starting to grow into a new tree.

Do-It-Yourself Plant Food

Have you ever been really hungry, but you were far away from any food? Wouldn't it be handy if you could make your own food from nothing but sunlight, air and water!
You can't, of course, but can you guess what can make its own food? That's right – plants!

Leaves help to carry food to every part of the plant.

A Special Name for Making Food

The way a plant makes food for itself is called **photosynthesis** (say: *fo-toe-sin-the-sis*).

Plants use their leaves to make food with only light from the Sun, **carbon dioxide** from the air and water from the soil. Tiny tubes in their leaves, called "veins", then carry the food to the rest of the plant. Plants use food to grow fruit or flowers, or to just … grow bigger!

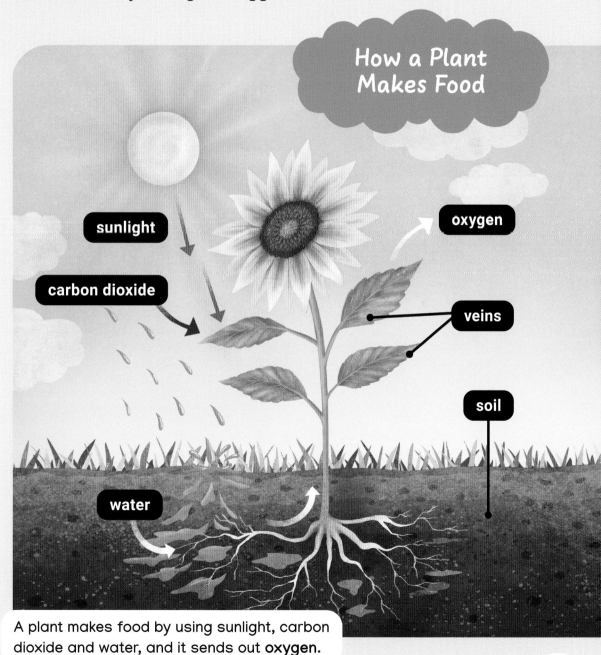

How a Plant Makes Food

sunlight

carbon dioxide

oxygen

veins

soil

water

A plant makes food by using sunlight, carbon dioxide and water, and it sends out **oxygen**.

Not all plants depend on their leaves for food. Some plants trap insects to eat instead. These meat-eating plants will feast on everything from slugs to spiders.

The Venus flytrap has special leaves that close like a mouth when a fly lands inside.

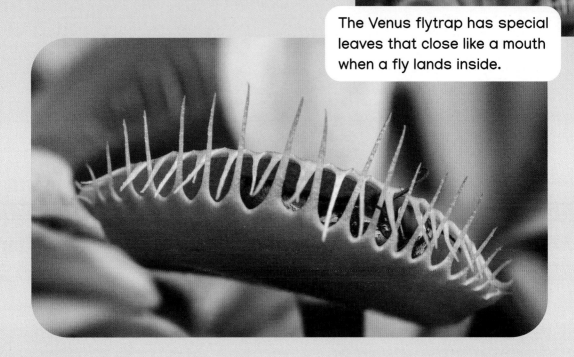

The sundew plant has sticky stalks that help it to catch insects.

How do these plants catch their prey? Well, let's look at how the pitcher plant does it. First, the plant's sweet-smelling nectar attracts a hungry insect. Then ... oops! The insect slides down a slippery tube and gets trapped in a watery pool inside the plant. When the body of the insect **rots**, the pitcher plant can feed on it.

A pitcher plant captures a beetle.

Stealing Prey

Some insects and spiders steal from pitcher plants. They can dive into the plant and pull out the trapped prey.

Thorns, Spikes and Clever Tricks

Although some plants eat insects, it's usually the plants themselves that are in danger of being eaten. Because they can't run away, plants need clever ways to protect themselves.

Some plants, like the cactus, grow thorns and spikes so that it's difficult for animals to eat them. *Ouch!*

Thorns on a cactus keep animals away.

Other plants try to trick their predators. The Swiss cheese plant has holes in its gigantic leaves. This sends a message to hungry caterpillars: "I've already been attacked. Try eating something else!"

The Swiss cheese plant has different patterns of holes in its leaves.

Look Who's Talking

It would be easy to laugh at the idea that plants can talk, but they really do have their own way of talking!

Some plants "speak" to each other through their roots underground. These plants have a **fungus** on their roots that talks to the roots of other plants about threats in the area. The fungus can even share food and water between the trees. It's like a secret dinner party!

How Trees Talk

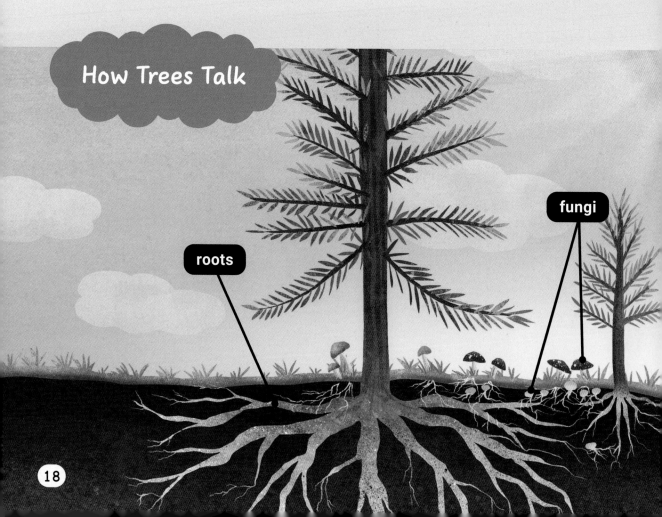

roots

fungi

This type of fungus can grow both above and under the ground.

Plants can "talk" to each other through fungi on their roots underground.

Tomato plants can send messages to insects, as well as to other tomato plants.

Here's how it happens.

 **Step 1** A caterpillar begins to munch on a tomato plant.

young tomato

caterpillar

This caterpillar is getting ready to eat a tomato plant.

Step 2 The tomato plant gives off a strong smell that says to the caterpillar, "Buzz off!"

When tomatoes are planted near each other, they can share smells.

Step 3 Tomato plants nearby can detect the smell from the first tomato plant. (Yes, really!) Then, they make their own smells to protect themselves from the caterpillar.

Step 4 Meat-eating insects are drawn to the smell and attack the caterpillar. The tomato plants are safe!

A wasp attacks a caterpillar.

It seems that plants have a secret world, where they are surprisingly busy. They spread their seeds far and wide, and they can fight off predators. They share secret messages, and some even trap their own food.

Perhaps if we watch the plants around us carefully, we might discover even more about their secret lives!

Try giving some plants a closer look today.

Grow your own plants to watch their secret lives!

You can learn more about plants on nature walks.

Glossary

attracts (*verb*)	gets interest or attention
carbon dioxide (*noun*)	a gas that plants take in from the air
fungus (*noun*)	a plant–like living thing that grows in soil and breaks down waste
nectar (*noun*)	a sweet liquid made by flowers
oxygen (*noun*)	a gas that plants put out, which helps keep other living things alive
photosynthesis (*noun*)	the way green plants use sunlight to make their own food
pollen (*noun*)	the powder found inside flowers that makes new seeds
pollination (*noun*)	the movement of pollen between plants to make seeds
reproduce (*verb*)	when plants and animals make new life
rots (*verb*)	slowly breaks down

Index